FEB '96

WI

Get set... GO!

Autumn

Ruth Thomson

Contents

CHILDRENS PRESS®
CHICAGO

It's autumn!

Autumn is a time of change.
The days become shorter and colder.
The leaves of trees and bushes turn
orange, yellow, and brown and fall off.

The hedges are bright
with rosehips and berries.
The ground is littered with acorns
and chestnuts and other seeds.

Many birds fly away
to warmer places for the winter.
Squirrels, mice, and chipmunks gather
stores of food and bury them.

Bats, frogs, snakes, and turtles
find a sheltered place.
They go into a deep sleep
called hibernation.

A leaf collection

Get ready

- ✔ Leaves
- ✔ Newspaper
- ✔ Heavy books
- ✔ Glue
- ✔ Scrapbook
- ✔ Felt-tip pen

. . . Get Set

Collect different kinds of fallen leaves.
Look carefully to find out
which trees they have come from.

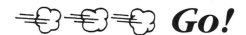 **Go!**

Lay the leaves between
two sheets of newspaper.
Put heavy books on top.
After two weeks, the leaves
will be flat and dry.
Glue them in a scrapbook and label them.

Cappadocian Maple

Hawthorn

Red Oak

Alder

Willow

Sweet Chestnut

Mountain Ash (Rowan)

Cherry

Autumn tree collage

Get ready

- ✔ Strong, thin paper
- ✔ Masking tape
- ✔ Crayons
- ✔ Different kinds of leaves
- ✔ Glue
- ✔ Blue paper
- ✔ Safety scissors

. . . Get Set

Tape thin paper to a tree trunk. Rub a crayon over it. A pattern of the tree's bark will appear. Dry some leaves (see page 4).

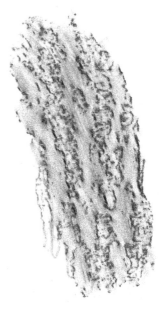

⇒⇔⇒⇔⇒⇔ *Go!*

Cut out a tree trunk shape from your bark rubbing. Glue it onto the blue paper. Glue on the dried leaves.

# A leafy face

Get ready

✔ Construction paper

✔ Leaves
✔ Glue

. . . Get Set

Dry some leaves (see page 4).
Group them by color, size, and shape.

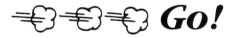 ## Go!

Arrange the leaves on the paper
in the shape of a face.
When you are happy with it,
glue the leaves to the paper.

Salt-dough models

Get ready

- ✔ 2 cups white flour
- ✔ 1 cup salt
- ✔ 1 cup cold water
- ✔ 2 tablespoons cooking oil
- ✔ Fork
- ✔ Food coloring
- ✔ Cookie sheet
- ✔ Mixing bowl

. . . Get Set

Stir ingredients in the bowl.
Press and knead the mixture with your hands.
Make small balls of dough.
Add drops of food coloring. Press and knead until the color is mixed in.

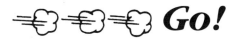 *Go!*

Shape the dough and cut and prick it with a fork to make patterns.
Ask an adult to help you bake it in the oven on a cookie sheet at 300 degrees for at least one hour.

# A fruit and seed collection

Get ready

✔ All kinds of fruits and seeds
  from trees, bushes, and flowers

. . . Get Set

Open some of the fruit to see
the seeds inside.
Keep pinecones in a warm, dry place.
Soon they will open, so you can see
their seeds.

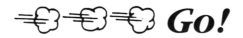 *Go!*

Find out the names of
your fruits and seeds.
Label your collection.

Sweet
Chestnuts

Beech fruits

Horse Chestnuts
(Buckeyes)

Plane seeds

Sycamore
wings

Ash
keys

Scotch Pine-
cones

Broom pods

Oak
acorns

Ivy seeds

Birch
seeds

Rosehips

See how seeds scatter

Get ready

✔ All kinds of fruits and seeds

. . . Get Set

Divide your collection into groups.

Winged seeds

ash *lime* *sycamore*

Nuts

beech nuts *buckeyes* *acorns*

Hooked fruits

burdock

yard grass

Plumed seeds

dandelion

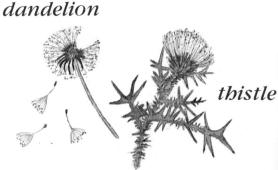

thistle

=❂=❂=❂ *Go!*

Throw winged seeds up in the air. Note how far they travel.

See how nuts are protected. Count the seeds in each case.

See what hooked fruits cling to. Try wood, fur, wool, plastic, and metal.

Blow a plumed seed head. Watch where the seeds go.

 # Seed picture

Get ready

✔ Flat seeds: ash, sycamore, elm, pumpkin, sunflower

✔ Construction paper
✔ Pencil
✔ Glue

. . . Get Set

Group your seeds by size and shape.
Draw the outline of a picture
lightly, in pencil.
Spread glue inside it.

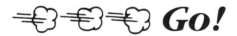 **Go!**

Stick seeds onto your picture.
Start at the edges and cover the outline.

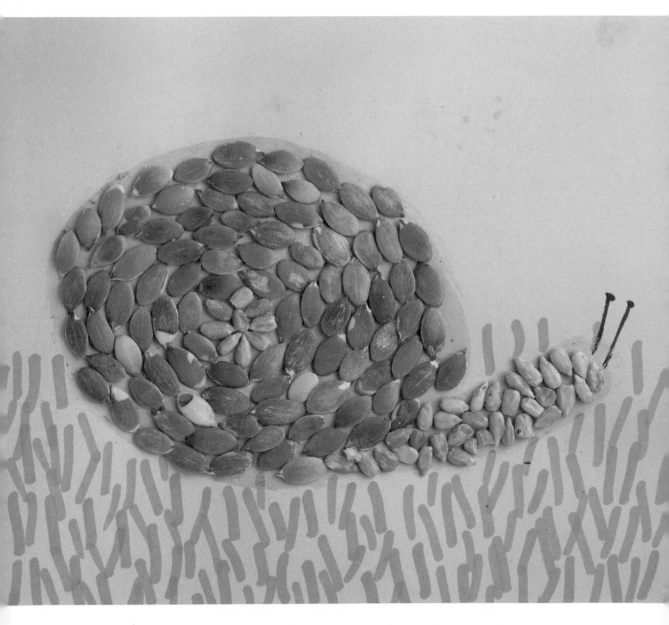

Autumn picture

Get ready

- ✔ Wood
  (3 feet by 1 inch)
- ✔ Nails
- ✔ Hammer
- ✔ Wood glue
- ✔ Wood stain
  or paint
- ✔ Stapler
- ✔ Leaves,
  twigs, seeds,
  berries
- ✔ String

. . . Get Set

Ask an adult to cut the wood into
four equal pieces.
Ask the adult to help you nail and
glue the pieces to make a frame.
Paint it or stain it.

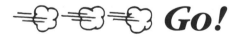 *Go!*

Staple leaves, twigs, and seeds
onto the back of the frame.
Hang berries on string.

Vegetable kebabs

Get ready

✔ Peppers
✔ Zucchini
✔ Mushrooms
✔ Cherry tomatoes

✔ Baby sweet corn
✔ Olive oil
✔ Lemon
✔ Lemon squeezer

✔ Knife
✔ Tablespoon
✔ Bowl
✔ Skewers

. . . Get Set

Ask an adult to cut the zucchini
and peppers into pieces.
Pour 3 tablespoons of oil into the bowl.
Ask an adult to cut the lemon in half.
Squeeze 3 tablespoons of lemon juice
into the bowl. Mix with the oil.
Soak the vegetables in this mixture for 2 hours.

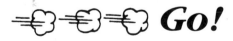 **Go!**

Stick the vegetables on skewers.
Ask an adult to help you grill them for 8 minutes,
turning often.

Woodland masks

Get ready

✔ Strips of newspaper

✔ Large balloon

✔ Wallpaper paste

✔ Safety scissors

✔ Paints and paintbrush

✔ Thin elastic

✔ Leaves, seeds, and feathers

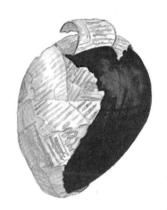

. . . Get Set

Paste several layers of newspaper strips over half a blown-up balloon. Let it dry for several days.

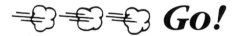 ## Go!

Take out the balloon.
Cut eye, nose, and mouth holes in the mask.
Paint it. Paste on leaves, seeds, and feathers.
Make a hole on each side.
Thread the elastic through and knot it.

Index

Photographic credits: Heather Angel, 15
(top l, top r, bottom r); Chris Fairclough
Colour Library, 3, 21; Peter Millard, 5, 7, 9,
11, 13, 17, 19

Editor: Pippa Pollard
Design: Ruth Levy
Cover design: Mike Davis
Artwork: Ruth Levy

Library of Congress Cataloging-in-Publication Data

Thomson, Ruth.
    Autumn / by Ruth Thomson.
        p.   cm. — (Get set— go!)
    Includes index.
    ISBN 0-516-07986-7
    1. Autumn—Juvenile literature. [1. Autumn. 2. Scientific
recreations.] I. Title. II. Series.
    QB637.7.T48   1994
    508—dc20   94-16940
                                                CIP
                                                AC

1994 Childrens Press® Edition
© 1993 Watts Books, London, New York, Sydney

24